Mending a Broken *Heart*

Mercedes Farmer

Copyright © 2018 by Mercedes Farmer

All rights reserved. No part of this publication may be reproduced, distributed, or transmitted in any form or by any means, including photocopying, recording, or other electronic or mechanical methods, without the prior written permission of the publisher, except in the case of brief quotations embodied in critical reviews and certain other noncommercial uses permitted by copyright law.

ISBN: 978-1-7320846-6-7

Liberation's Publishing LLC
West Point, Mississippi
www.liberationspublishing.com

Dedicated to my 5 year-old self

Contents

Preface vii
Introduction 9
The Poem that Describes My Life 15
My Heartbreak 18
My Grandmother 19
Please Listen to Me 21
I'm Offering This To You 23
A Poem to Our Parents 25
The Mother I Wish Was Mine (In My Dreams) . 27
My Farewell to the Class of 2006 28
Remembering Stephanie Tubbs Jones 30
History Has Been Made: President Barack Obama
.... 32
Big Mama's Passing 34
We Are First: Celebrating Women 36
A Lookback: A Year after Whitney Houston's
Death 38
My Way Out 40
The Name of Jesus 42
Being Her True Self 43
This Day Means Nothing 45
Untitled 48
The Truth 49

Is Love Enough? 51
A Year Without You 53
Nighttime Thoughts 55
Justice for Trayvon Martin...57
Feelings of Hope..59
Unforgettable Dad 60
The Reality I'm Facing...62
Difficulties of Life and the Aftermath........................64
The New America 67
Pleading for That One to Stay.....................................70
Farewell to The Obamas 72

Preface

One day, during my first week as Principal of John F. Kennedy High School, a young girl walked into my office, sat down and announced that she was a sophomore and that she wanted to introduce herself to me. I was immediately impressed and rather amused by her strong demeanor and confident, bubbly personality. Little did either of us know that we were related by marriage and that our relationship would grow into one of mutual respect, admiration and love.

It is a rare thing for an educator to be able to see the seed they have planted come to fruition. It is equally rare for someone to be both the victim and the victor at the same time! This collection of verses, this mass of poetry and prose, this conglomeration of painful and joyful transparency, speaks to the heart of every youth who has had to I overcome life in order to simply live.

Thank you Mercedes Farmer for reaching out to us by baring your soul. Thank you for your grace and your willingness to speak your truth so beautifully. Thank you for your courage to stand up and to not forget that we lead by being servants to others...to lead is to love!

Congratulations to a born leader who has so much love yet to give!

Your Forever Principal, Play Mom and Friend,
Charita Crockrom Sullivan

Mercedes Farmer

Introduction

I wasn't sure how I wanted to present this book of poems to my readers. I searched non-stop working within myself to come up with ideas for this book. One night I was sitting at home and an idea hit me; "Why don't I write a letter to my younger self?" "What age? I wasn't sure. My first thought was to write a letter to my ten year old self. Then I thought, "maybe to my seven year old self." Finally around midnight one night, I decided on my five year old self.

This age I remember vividly; as I look back over my life, I realize that this age was the age when things started to unravel for me. What I hope that people take away from this book of poems is healing. We all have gone through trials in this thing called life (if you haven't-keep living) but we all have power to overcome whatever it is. Admitting that there are stumbling blocks that occur on our way to our destiny, can be the thing that helps carry us to our destiny.

I hope this book helps some young girl or boy, who thinks it's too late, love themselves more than the hate they may feel for someone else; for love conquers hate.

Mercedes Farmer

Dear Five Year Old Mercedes,

There are things that you will endure at a very young age. Your heart will be broken before you realize that broken hearts exist. There are things that you will not understand and you will find yourself asking "Why me?". You will find ways to escape this roller coaster called life. You will endure sexual assault, rape, neglect, abandonment and that's all by the age of eleven. You will fall into a deep depression, enter a mental hospital and develop an extraordinary love for painkillers, leading to an addiction that you just can't seem to shake. You just want the pain to stop.

You will work hard fighting to fit in and receive love from anyone; hoping that this will fill a void in your heart from your own mother not loving you (heads up, she will stop loving and liking you in two years so enjoy the moments now). You will spend your teenage and most of your twenties catering to others; constantly taking care of others needs and wants, still trying to give what you have lacked but no one will be returning the favor. The disappointment that you will come into contact with will cause you to be less confident in yourself. However, through it all, you master staying functional and keep a smile on your face but you will cry yourself to sleep many nights.

I'm writing this to encourage you not to give up. Although it will get rough, and believe me, it will get rough, you will develop an inner strength that is so huge that it will allow you to believe you are someone and that you do matter. Your love for writing will save you from keeping those suicidal thoughts from sinking deep into your mind. Your admiration for music and lyrics will allow you to enter into another world getting lost in the rhythms and melodies so that you don't have to face your own reality. You will learn to live your life for yourself and not for anyone else. You will grow a closer relationship with God, realizing it was He who took care of you all along.

Three things to remember:
1) Be self-full: Take care of you first.
2) Don't worry about what others say or think: allow yourself to be who it is you want to be.
3) Be confident. You are smart. You are you!

Don't be fearful; for God did not give us a spirit of fear!!!

With love and peace,
Your Twenty Nine Year Old Self.

Mending a Broken Heart

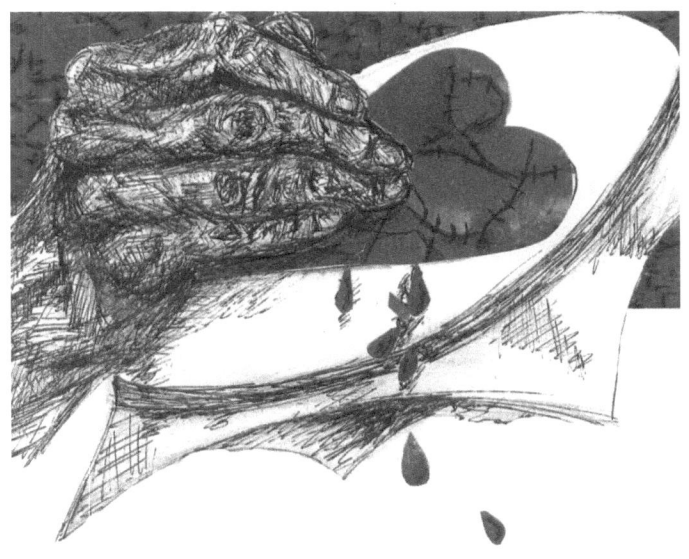

Mercedes Farmer

The Poem that Describes My Life
Age 13 December 6, 2001

I'm going down

'cause no one's around

No one's around to do the things I wanna do.

No one's around to care the way I need them to.
Never in my life did I have positive things to walk about.

Never in my life did I have positive things to talk about.

I guess I'm in this world alone

Not having love or power to heal my soul.

What am I going to do?

My mom and dad both kicked me out and now I feel so blue.

People don't understand the stuff I go through

Maybe one day I will have someone to talk to discuss my problems,

To help me get through the sorrow and pain to heal my heart before it begins to rain

Will I live on the streets?

Will I have food to eat?

Will I have the chance to depend on someone

or will I look back over my life and say "OH NO?!"

I'm only 13 and I've been through so much.

Will this change or will I treat my kids the same way?

Every night I try not to cry but those tears keep running right out of my eyes.

I think about the same things over and over;

the abuse, the name calling, the backstabbing, the murder.

Will I change?

Will this change?

Will I always be in the rain?

Will the dreams I have go up in flames?

Will the dreams of becoming a singer, dancer or artist still be the things I wanna do or will my family turn their backs on me saying "I don't care what she do?"

This world is getting crazy

Family put family down

Family put family out

but what about me, will I have the time?

When I get older, will I look back over my life and laugh or will the pain hurt too bad?

Will The Lord comfort my heart to keep me from crying or will I have to live with a foster parent to keep me from dying?

Will my family turn their back on me or will my

friends turn their backs on me?

I guess I'll have to see, when the hands on the clock turn back again!

My Heartbreak

Age 13 January 29, 2002

In life, people are going to turn your world upside down.

They are going to lie to you, hurt you and make your cry.

They are going to abuse you, neglect you and harm you (in every way possible)

They are going to make you feel worthless, unwanted and unloved.

They are going to kick you while you're standing and kick you harder when you are down.

They are going to call you names, tell you that you won't make it and make you look over your life (in

all the wrong ways).

They will rape you; bringing you down to your lowest points, physically, mentally, emotionally and

spiritually.

They will steal from you. Murder you.

Still telling you over and over again how much they love you!

Watch these people!

They are not trustworthy!

My Grandmother
Age 15 December 21, 2003

On this Christmas Day I'm going to read this poem
For it's all about my grandmother, who is a very special one.
Big Mama is what I've called her for 15 years.
Big Mama is the air of this family of which everyone breathes.
She's like the angel of our Christmas tree,
the Santa with little money
my grandmother which everyone loves; the one that's sweeter than honey.
As long as I've known her, I can say one thing;
she says whatever she feels and that's how I hope to be.
I can't speak for everyone but I can speak for me.
Without my grandmother, I do not know where I would be.
Her arms are always open when I need a helping hand.
Today this poem was made for her
to let my grandmother know
I'll love her always and forever more.

For all those who have a loving, warmhearted, caring grandmother like me

Remember she's the best grandmother, a grandmother can be.

Please Listen to Me
Age 15 March 8, 2004

My poems are my light

They teaches me how to fight.

How to fight the emotions I have.

How to make myself laugh.

People usually don't care what I go through and at times they don't know what to do.

I write the poems to let me know,

that someone really loves me so but who?

I'm not really sure.

If I could have three things in the world it would be: love, peace and guidance.

For my family won't always be around to help me with my problems.

It's not like this family knows anything about me and at times I'm sure they often pray to God and tell

Him about it.

Sometimes I don't know what is going on with me or who exactly am I turning out to be.

My faith is wrong and the hope is gone and, yet, I'm still all alone.

Without a mother, am I going down? Maybe I will have time to turn my life around.

Is it too late?

Lord please help and comfort my soul.

Please, oh please, make me whole.

Teach me, teach me because I need you and without you there is nothing I can do.

I'm Offering This To You
Age 16 May 20, 2004

I am offering this poem to you

since I have nothing else to give

keep it like a flower

when you need to smell a scent

or like a fresh, summer day in the middle of May

-I love you

I have nothing else to give you

so it is a pitcher full of ice tea

to keep you cool in the summer

a hat to go over your head

to keep the sun out of your face

-I love you-

Keep it, treasure this as you would

if you were missing me and needed love;

in the midst of rain when it becomes moist

and in the middle of your heart

tucked away is my love

that keeps you warm inside and I will never leave you

that where you go

I will be also

-I love you

It's all I have to give

to let you know my love is deep in your heart.

When the world outside no longer cares if you remember me so

-I love you

A Poem to Our Parents
Age 17 (Senior Parent Night at John F Kennedy High School) October 27, 2005

Our parents are the ones who gives us life to start

They help us understand the goodness that we are.

Through the good, bad, sunshine and rain,

We can always count on our parents to help us get through sorrow and pain.

Everything we do reflects on our parents.

No matter what the outcome is we will always cherish;

Cherish all the love they gave throughout the years and all the times they wiped away the tears.

If for some reason you do not have your parents

Take time to thank those who have enlightened;

enlightened your way and touched your lives.

Have taken you under their wings and made sure everything was alright.

As much as I would like to go on and on,

Senior Parents, we truly hope you have enjoyed this time.

And on behalf of the students I would like to say,

We thank our parents for helping us

become what we are today!!!

The Mother I Wish Was Mine (In My Dreams)
Age 17 December 2, 2005

Her hugs lets me know that I am so loved.

Her kisses are as sweet as her hugs.

Her voice is from a mother to my ears and I love when she yells at me because it shows how much she cares.

She shows me so much in so many ways.

I appreciate having her every day.

She's the mother I wish to have

She's the light that shows me the right path.

I love her and everything that comes with it.

I love calling her "Mommy". She gives me so much guidance.

She's an angel sent from the Heavens above.

I'm just innocent, looking for love.

Everyone knows!

Was I a mistake? Not in her eyes.

Wow, she is such an incredible mom.

Only thing I ask is that she stay my mom forever.

Never let anyone come between this relationship I plan to cherish.

My Farewell to the Class of 2006
Age 17 (John F. Kennedy's Graduation) April 24, 2006

Never stop dreaming those really BIG dreams.

Never lose sight of who you are within.

Never say you are going off to college and won't be back.

Try not to disappoint anyone, including yourself!

Never forget who told you not to sell yourself short.

Never forget who was there when you needed someone.

Never forget that teacher, counselor, principal or friend who showed so much interest in you.

Never let go of who you are and what you want to do.

Always hold close to your heart these last four years we shared.

Keep happy thoughts in your mind and show others how much you care.

Go off into the world and be something others can look up to.

If you cannot touch the stars,

there's always the moon!

Always love yourself; through the thick and thin
and it's okay to make a mistake
just don't do the same again!
Remember things happen for a reason; whether good or bad
So if you do not get what you want in life
be glad of what you have.
Remember God is everything you need and want
He is the light of your path when it seems to get dark.
What I liked best about this class was the ability to have fun
but in life remember to have fun whenever the job is done.
Before I end this special poem,
I want to leave the Class of 2006 with a little advice;
Think about the things you do
courses you take and moves you make
for where you go others will end up too.
Be a role model, friend and teacher too!!
-Congratulations,
Good Luck & God Bless you all

Remembering Stephanie Tubbs Jones

Age 20 August 21, 2008

Cleveland has lost an advocate.

Ohio has lost and icon.

This nation has lost a hard worker.

Everyone has lost a friend.

If I could remember one thing about Stephanie, it would be her smile.

Just how BIG and bright it was and how her smile made me smile.

She was involved in everything and truly loved people.

She took time to stop by local schools to say "Hello" to students and teachers.

Her spirit filled a room.

Her attitude changed my mood.

Her heart was BIG and filled with love.

She was a blessing sent from the Heavens above.

Cleveland has not only lost an advocate; we have lost a supporter.

Ohio has not only lost an icon; we have lost a legend.

This nation has not only lost a hard worker; we have lost a champion.

Everyone has lost a friend.

History Has Been Made: President Barack Obama
Age 20 November 5, 2008

On November 4, 2008 history was made!!

For those of us who voted, know the results of this day.

Many people including me cried happy tears because this was a beautiful sight to see.

The results were coming fast and Obama was in the lead.

I am happy that my grandmother is around to see such a beautiful thing.

For she has seen many things in her lifetime; some good and some bad but she never thought in a

million years that she would see this day.

When I heard that Obama had won Ohio, my heart skipped a beat.

WOW! An African American man? We have made history!!

No matter what party you are for; Republican or Democrat

we must know that we are all Americans and our President needs us.

Barack Obama, an intelligent person and a

wonderful family man;

He loves his family and Michelle is his #1 fan.

I am happy to say that I voted to help elect Barack Obama.

I can't wait til the day I tell my children about the day history was made.

For all of you who have supported Obama

Please let's continue…

and once he gets into the White House, let's pray that God will protect and keep him.

We are all Americans no matter our color, age or gender.

Barack Obama, the first black president

…this is how we made history.

~Celebrate~

Big Mama's Passing
Age 24 June 21, 2012

There have been many times in my life when life seemed unfair.

I have cried and asked God, why was I here.

He gave me something special.

He gave me hope.

He told me that life was not over;

that it had just begun.

Thirteen years ago, my brother and I were dropped off on Big Mama's front porch.

She began to care for us as if we were her own.

She taught me how to keep God first; pray, seek and find love in Him.

She taught me how to say please and thank you and to always have respect for me.

She taught me how to have faith in me; to never quit on anything.

I remember her telling me about my attitude; how hateful and stubborn I can be and although she never

had to whoop me, her looks of disappointment were enough for me.

I will miss eating out of her plate, even though I

could have gotten my own.

I will miss jumping in her bed and being wrapped up in her arms.

I will miss her at Family Fun Night, buying all the Christmas gifts with Monopoly Money.

My grandmother had a kind heart and I never felt lonely.

To my family who I know will miss her so much; miss her laughs, miss her talks, miss her way of

words and her unconditional love, but

We must know that her time was up and God carried her home.

We shall never forget our individual memories we've shared with her for Big Mama will always have a

special place in our hearts.

We miss you dearly and love you always

We Are First: Celebrating Women
Age 25 February 7, 2013

Many time in history men played great roles but there are women in history that got the job done.

There are so many women in history who carried out such important duties.

I will name a few who showed their beauty.

First African American woman to earn a BA was Mary Jane Patterson from Oberlin College and who is responsible for our hair being so pretty?

The wonderful Madam CJ Walker

Dr. Mae Jemison was the first black female astronaut in NASA history

and later this year Rosa Parks will become the first African American woman with a statue on Capitol Hill.

First black U.S. Secretary of State- Condoleeza Rice.

Hattie McDaniel won the first Oscar for 'Gone with the Wind'. Wow, now that's nice!!

First female Grammy Award winner was Ella Fitzgerald

and in 1984 the crown was given to Vanessa Williams for Miss America.

The Queen of Daytime Talk Shows- Oprah Winfrey.

She became the first black woman television host in 1986.

Shirley Chisholm was the first black woman to serve in Congress in 1969 and Toni Morrison wrote great literature and won the Noble Peace Prize.

In 2008, we made things greater when Michelle Obama became our first black First Lady.

What will hold next for women in our future?

In 2016, could we have a President by the name of Hillary Clinton?

There are a lot of things left for us to do.

So get up, get out and do something new.

Chaka Khan and Whitney Houston acknowledged that we are 'Every Woman'

I say this to women both old and young; rather you are black or white, rich or poor.

Life may be hard and issues may rise but we have the ability to make it far.

We are smart and beautiful and intelligent too. We can do anything we put our minds to do.

A Lookback: A Year after Whitney Houston's Death

Age 25 February 8, 2013

It was a year ago on February 11th when I received that horrible news.

That the one person who I loved so much was gone and I felt so blue.

The music stopped that night for me as I cried for days, weeks and months.

My heart was filled with much grief and pain.

I prayed I would move on.

Life, as a child was pretty rough.

I hated me and who I was.

Whitney's songs gave me strength and power.

Her songs allowed me to end such sorrow.

Her songs allowed me to escape from my world; my world of abuse and neglect was all I had known.

But when 'The Greatest Love of All' soared through my soul

I felt as though I was wrapped up in Whitney's arms.

I remember watching CNN and asking God "Why?"

Why would He take the person He gave to me, the one that kept me from dying.

Months went by and I felt a little bit better but every time I heard her music, saw her movies or read a magazine, my heart became heavy.

I felt like I had lost a close family member and just like the song asks, "Where Do Broken Hearts Go?"

To be honest, I don't think I will ever know

I can't imagine her mother's and daughter's pain; life for them, I know, will never be the same.

There will never be another artist who did what she did for me.

There will never be another singer who has fulfilled that void for me.

Now because of Whitney, I know my own strength.

Is there another great singer and artist in the world?

As for me, I say NO!

The life, the music, the legacy will forever live on.

"I Will Always Love You"

My Way Out
Age 25 March 1, 2013

Am I addicted to prescription drugs?

Well I may be!

Life can be unbearable and it's hard to be me.

I want to be better at whatever I attempt to do.

I thought I would be at that place now that I can start anew

Depression is taking over me; it's deep, dark and blue.

I want to be through with it but it keeps pulling me through it.

Through the pits of sorrow and pain from life's uninvited events.

Through the current situations of the here and nows that I can't seem to shake.

My choice of prescription drugs give me a way out away from the world and the many things going on

I can sleep time away and not have others problems take over.

I'm only human

I'm so very young

I can function well, and yet, I am so alone!

I have reached out for help from many who are

around

but I guess they thought this wasn't an issue BIG enough to solve.

I never stop praying and reading The Word.

God never stopped loving me and I am happy for this so.

He knows my struggles.

He knows my doubts.

I know that prescription drugs are my temporary way out

~I miss me~

The Name of Jesus
Age 25- April 2, 2013

It's something about the name of Jesus that we love so much

It's something about His name that keeps us coming back for more.

There is no one else in the world that we can call a friend;

He protects us. He loves us. He is always there.

Are you encouraged?

Do you believe His Word is true?

He answers our calls and hears our cries.

He holds us when we're lonely, late at night.

We must thank Him in advance for those things He will do.

There is no one else in this universe we should adore more than Him!

Being Her True Self
Age 25 - April 19, 2013

There has never been a person that I have met.

That has touched my heart and soul with laughter…who gives me their best.

I appreciate the moments I have had thus far with them.

I can honestly say they love me for me.

I get upset, sometimes, for the things they say.

They have never once apologized for telling me the right way.

The truth is all they know.

I never had someone in my life to tell me such so.

I love them as if I had them my whole life.

They're the people I wish I had through my ups and downs.

They listen to my happiness and the pain I feel inside and if I get too crazy, they are not fearful in helping me get my mind right.

I love their honesty.

Their sense of humor.

Their way of making me stop and think.

Their no-nonsense attitude and the love they show unconditionally.

God gives us the right people at the right times in our lives.

I am so grateful for this time He has given me with them.

They keep me grounded,

thinking,

laughing

and crying.

There is nothing in this world I wouldn't do for them.

They become the sunshine when my life seems dark.

I just love them...with all my heart.

This Day Means Nothing
Age 25 May 12, 2013

Mother's Day has never been the same for me.

It's still very hurtful for me.

I still don't understand what it is I have done to make my mom not want to be a mom and love me so much.

I often think about what I could have done differently.

Should I have kept my mouth closed and not tell her that her husband was raping me?

Does she think about me on my birthday?

Does she think about me on a Tuesday?

Does she think about me on Christmas day?

Does she think about me on any day?

Life, for me, has never been the same since the day I was forced to give my childhood away.

How could one have a child and not love and care for her?

In the last 14 years I've felt like an orphan.

There are still a lot of issues that I am dealing with inside like trust and truth and who I am and am I alive inside?

I wanted things to be better by the time I turned

25 but somehow I keep having the same problems.

I really want God's arms to wrap around me so tightly.

I really want to remove myself from people who won't help me move higher.

For years I thought she would come back

to show me the love I felt I lacked

but after a year, there was no luck

then I felt like I was stuck in bitterness, unforgiveness, lies, murder and deceit.

Hurt, pain, sorrow and grief.

Where does this leave me at this very hour?

The things I have named keep weighing me down!

Because of such hurt and because of such pain

I have not yet washed away my abuser's name.

How could my childhood be stolen from me.

Children are supposed to have love, laughter, peace and be free.

As for me, I am still bonded by misery

trying to work through and struggle to get out wickedness.

Yes, life was unfair. I was dealt the wrong hand but there has to be a reason why I am still alive;

fighting this fight, watching joy end the sorrow.

Only time will tell what my future holds.

Hugs, love, laughter and peace are the things I have always longed for.

I deserve better, yes I know

but on this Mother's Day, I feel so alone!!

Untitled

Age 25 May 14, 2013

Through pain and destruction, lies and unfaithfulness.

I'm still here.

Through sickness and rain, bitterness and guilt.

I'm still here.

While living in this moment, I often think could life had been any better for me?

Of course!! I could've had the perfect life with two loving parents; cooking and cleaning and constantly caring.

They could have been the ideal parents, the ones I could talk to; when problems arose I know who I could run to.

I often think about how life could have been different.

If I had known what to do from the very beginning.

But I have to let it go.

Thinking too hard won't change the past.

I gotta get it together and I gotta make it fast.

Life could have been way worse!!

The Truth
Age 25 June 5, 2013

The truth is I love you too much to let things change.

The truth is our relationship is beyond anything I have ever dreamed of.

The truth is you are the ONLY person I have shared my dreams and thoughts with.

The truth is you make me feel love again.

I think about those days when my feelings were hurt.

When life knocked me down and pushed me in the dirt.

I think about how I wish you were there to wipe away the tears; to show how much you cared.

The truth is I wish we were more than just this.

The truth is I wish I could share my secrets of regrets.

I wish you knew me more than the smile that I show.

I wish I didn't feel unworthy of the love you let grow.

The truth is I wish I was more like yours; there are times when I feel like you don't like me no more.

The truth is you are the best thing going on right

now.

Two and a half years ago I was ready to give up and die but God stepped in right on time and gave me

His precious prize.

Truth is there is nothing I would not do for you.

My heart overflows with humanity and gratitude.

You are that positive reinforcement that I waited for.

My life has been on track since walking through this door.

Truth is this has to stay forever and forever.

Truth is this is the longest, effective relationship I have had ever.

I just thank God for the blessings He gives.

From me to you I thank you for accepting who I am.

Is Love Enough?
Age 25 June 8, 2013

Do I love me enough to know that wrong is wrong?

Do I love me enough to let people go on and go?

Do I love me enough to not let people take over my soul?

Do I love me enough to not let evilness take over me as a whole?

Do I love me enough to know when enough is enough?

Do I love me enough to not let the devil come and steal my stuff?

I know that the enemy comes to kill, steal and destroy but do I love me enough to get up and walk strong?

Life has played some dirty tricks on me.

It has left me helpless and feeling unfree.

It has stolen life's precious gifts from me but do I love me enough to set myself free?

Free from the tears I cry at night.

Free from the bitterness I keep inside.

Free from the drugs I use to cope with the pain.

Free from the thoughts I think about all day.

I wish I could be better than I am.

I want people to stop dictating my life plans.

I know there is a purpose for my life.

The fact that He allowed me to live through such heartache and strife says a lot about who He says I am

One touch from Him can, indeed, make me whole.

Sometimes I ask why did He allow me to go on.

He loves me enough to answer when I am calling.

He loves me enough to know what I need before I need it.

He loves me enough to watch over me when I'm sleeping.

He loves me enough to tell me "no" and "wait"

He loves me enough to wipe the tears from my heart and face.

He is a wonderful God

Prince of Peace

What I long for is a relationship and to walk deeply in Him

I can!!

        Just keep seeking Him.

A Year Without You
Age 25 June 23, 2013

In the loving memory of Lula Farmer

whom I love and miss with all my power.

A year has passed and although my grief has gotten better

My hunger for her has grown greater.

This last year has really been a struggle

I fell on hard times and had no comfort.

I prayed and asked God how can this get better?

How can my life go on with this great depression?

I believe He spoke to me and gave me something to hold on to.

There were many times in my life when I wanted to leave but after that dosage of medication,

He allowed my grandmother to show up in my dreams;

where she still gave me guidance, love, encouragement and advice

She still tells me where I should and should not go and how I should be living a peaceful life.

Yes, it's been a year.

I still laugh. I still cry

but I believe she is a guardian angel standing right

by my side!!

Nighttime Thoughts
Age 25 June 24, 2013

As I lay back and think how my life could've been.

If I had sought Him first the Kingdom

What would life have been.

We know that God lets all things happen for a reason but I need a breakthrough.

I'm ready for my season.

I know it is on the way.

I will not doubt what He say.

He wants me to be the best but for some reason, I feel, I keep failing His test.

The door is there just waiting to be opened

He wants me to walk through it with power and be anointed.

Some people will go with me and some will not.

Some will be happy for me and, well, others will not.

Resist the devil and he will flee.

God is my shield. He will NEVER leave.

I am so excited about what the future holds.

Faith without works is dead so I better get going.

My past doesn't define who I am or the things that I will do.

With God all things are possible.
How do I know?
Because His Word is true!!!

Justice for Trayvon Martin
Age 25 July 13, 2013

Where do broken hearts go?

Is the question all over the world.

The world is broken and torn because, yet again, justice was not served

Six women served on jury and deliberated for 16 hours.

How could they let Zimmerman go?

How could they let him have power?

My heart is broken

They failed us all

That could've been our son or brother walking to that corner store.

Since when does ice tea and skittles serve as weapons?

When will we, as people, learn our lessons?

The lessons of racism;

growing up as a black man and woman in today's time.

The great leaders of our world tried to warn us

that this wouldn't be over by far.

My question, like others all over, is why wasn't justice served?

Why was this family not put at peace, knowing that their son's murderer was is set free.

So this is what it means to stand your ground for a 17 year old boy to be gunned down

how could Zimmerman live with himself knowing he shot and killed a young man;

whose future is forever gone and the family left in pain.

To The Martin Family,

just know that sorrow does not last forever.

That The Lord knows what He is doing.

He is a shield in the time of a storm.

Although we do not know the answers, we just keep asking why.

The world all over is in disbelief but some of us are not surprised.

We will continue to pray and lift you up

Wherever we are all over the globe.

For The Lord is our Shepherd and He takes care of us so.

We must trust and believe that HIS justice will be served!!

Feelings of Hope
Age 25 November 1, 2013

The only one who makes me feel weak then turns around and make me feel strong.

How can I be so right and, yet, still so wrong?

The only one who can make me cry and laugh within a few seconds.

Sometimes when I need an ear to hear, I'm not sure if you're listening.

I value your opinion from beginning to end.

I may not seem like I'm listening but, yes, I got it.

Life, right now, is a struggle and I believe God is giving me what I need;

To make it across this journey and I was hoping you would stand with me…

To love, care and support through good and bad times.

To speak only good things and never tell me lies

To lift me up when I'm feeling down

When I need a friend, can I count on you to be around??!!!

Unforgettable Dad
Age 25 March 9, 2014

I haven't been able to sleep these last few nights.

On the one night I was able to sleep, The Lord woke me up about 3AM

I believe He told me to get up and write.

Now, I was fighting this because I was finally sleeping but I know He would give me rest again.

So I did what anyone would do when The Lord speaks,

I started writing at 3AM.

When daddy and I were preparing for this moment,

I knew this day would come.

However, I never thought he'd leave so fast after I released and let him go.

No, he wasn't the best at times

and neither was he the worse

but I am blessed for the time we spent; especially in these last few months.

I will miss his unforgettable stories, his memories of growing up as a child, his very dramatic ways and

how his sense of humor was often dry.

I will miss him humming to songs because he did

not know the words.

I will miss him giving me advice even when I did not ask him at all.

I will miss him making me read the newspaper and The Daily Bread.

I will always remember when he started to teach me how to drive and how much he really cared.

There are people here who knew just how funny daddy could be

There were times when he was not so funny to me.

We laughed a lot these past months about many many things but the sicker he got, the laughter stopped

Things got extremely intense as the days went by.

I knew it was only a matter of time before my dad would die.

Am I sad? Of course, only because I will miss him dearly.

But I am very grateful and thankful unto God that daddy's suffering has ended.

The Reality I'm Facing
Age 26 August 4, 2014

When I think about the times I have wasted on people and things, I get mad at myself.

When I think about the lies I believed, I get disappointed in myself.

When I think about the people I put first and they put me last, I am hurt.

When I think about my life and the stupid choices I've made, I am disgusted with myself.

Since I can remember I have always tried to gain people's love.

Love from those who hated me, talked about me, lied on me.

Love from those who hurt me, abused me and destroyed me.

Love from those who walked on me, dumped me and left me alone.

It's amazing the hurtful things people will do in the name of love.

I'm finally getting that love don't love me anymore.

But did it love me before?

It's hard to say.

My wounds are still sore.

I am trying hard to let go of past hurts; those things seems to keep showing up in my present thoughts.

Difficulties of Life and the Aftermath
Age 27 July 19, 2015

I have experienced a whole lot in my life of which I did not deserve

After coming through each storm, all I really wanted was love.

I use to want the approval of my mother; I wanted her to see me as her daughter.

I wanted her love, protection and guidance but I never received any.

I was never more to her, just like a stranger on the street.

How can she allow her boyfriend to rape me and take my innocence?

How could she allow his seed to grow within me?

How could she not believe me and throw me away?

How could she still hate me 'til this very day?

Then I grew up and realized that our relationship will never be.

So I went out and found people who I thought would validate me.

I only saw what I wanted and accepted the love that they give but now I realize the love given was never for my gain.

Some people pitied me and some used me.

Some people thought I wouldn't make it without them.

I have come to understand now that I was lied to by so many people.

These people never saw me for me, just for what I could be to them.

I didn't realize where my life was heading until my dad took sick.

Those same people who claimed to love me were nowhere near.

They didn't call or visit or ask "Is there anything I can do?"

People are always about themselves until they need someone to use.

When my daddy died, it truly grew me up.

I realized that so many people were not who they said they were.

I have grown into who I am and learned to live my life.

People will tell you what you want to hear and expect you to be alright.

I am not that same girl, hurt, bitter or angry.

I have surrounded myself with people who allow me to be greater.

I am grateful for who I am and the path it took to

get here.

God is my everything and more and because of that I can go on!

The New America
Age 28 July 7, 2016

When you think about the America we live in and the issues we see everyday

When black lives can be taken and police have nothing to say.

When the world we wake up to

can cover the news of senseless murders

What can we do, as a nation, to cover each other?

We are only through half the year and there have been so many killings of black lives, fathers, brothers,

sons and they keep saying we matter?

But how can we when we are worried about emails of Hillary?

It's a sad day to see when you are fearful to bring a child into this world.

Because you don't know how to raise them; to be afraid of authority and all.

When you can be doing something right and still be gunned down like a dog

I thought we were doing better in this country.

I wanted us to love each other more.

I thought I would see the day when racism didn't take over our hearts and souls.

Everyone is in an outrage; posting things on social media talking about "we should take a stand"

but it's the same things being repeated.

We're only pissed in that moment; maybe a week or two.

Then we go back to our lives as if it's nothing new.

It's a repeated cycle in this country now-

I'm not suggesting we disrespect police but when will we open our eyes?

Over 100 black lives taken this year and it is only July

How many more families will mourn their loved ones before we actually rise?

I think about my own brother, driving up and down the highways; just trying to make a living.

I don't want us to be fearful but that's the time we're in.

This world is going backwards.

Civil Rights leaders have died for us to have opportunities

The NRA should be on top of this.

Republicans and Democrats should come together to stop this.

How many murders will happen from police and each other before we actually decide

that this is not the way we want to live...

We want justice and we want it now!!!

Pleading for That One to Stay
Age 28 September 12, 2016

I hurt you. I know.

Your feelings are sore.

My mind is blown.

That I hurt you so…

You have been by my side

My ride or die!!

My counselor, my friend, my guide.

I am extremely mad at myself for what I have done.

You have been the only one I can call on.

Have I ruined this relationship?

This, that I have adored?

The love, peace and advice you give, can it be restored?

I feel so stupid that I cannot breathe.

My heart is broken and it won't stop bleeding.

You are different from others in every single way.

You have been that person I prayed that I would have one day.

I am hoping and praying that you won't leave my life.

Stick it out with me, just one more time.

Help me be a better person and all.
Love me more than the hate overall.
I know you care and I care too.
Don't walk away from me, leaving me feeling blue.
If you leave me, I will feel alone.
I have never felt the love that you give me before.
Lord, allow your will to be done in this relationship.
You know how much I care and want to be forgiven.
I apologize for all I have done.
My heart is sincere and filled with love.
God, please make it better and help me to grow.
I really am sorry for what I have done.

Farewell to The Obamas
Age 28 January 10, 2017

Farewell to The First Family

WOW! Eight years have gone by fast.

Barack, Michelle, Malia, Sasha, Bo and Sunny are all saying good-bye!!!

I get choked up and eyes get filled

just thinking about this family and how it's all coming to an end.

President Obama was the first President I had ever voted for.

I cried so hard when he won.

Now, I'm crying to see him go.

I have never been so mesmerized by such wonderful people

Michelle's wit, class, grace, intelligence

Oh! how I wish I could meet her.

Although they are leaving The White House to start life anew

I only send the best of wishes to each and every one of you.

So, as the new guy enters The White House

it's very hard to believe.

I just want to say thanks to The First Family

for being the best role model
any family can be.

Mercedes Farmer

ABOUT THE AUTHOR

Mercedes Farmer is a Cleveland native whose passion for poetry and writing has been the avenue of escape from pain of growing up without the mother she had known and loved.

Rescued by her grandmother from a cold existence and bolstered by a father's love, Mercedes' collection of poems is a triumph over depression and abandonment and a testament to the strength of the human soul.

Mercedes Farmer

www.ingramcontent.com/pod-product-compliance
Lightning Source LLC
Chambersburg PA
CBHW060504080526
44584CB00015B/1547